QUARANTINE

CONFESSIONS

3

aka
(for better or worse)

The Ballad of Billy Ancaster

BILLY BLOWS IT

is the ending to this one,

but I figured I'd do it different

because we're in month comma who-
cares

of a pandemic that won't end

and no one wants to read about
cases

and chronology

and since formatting was never
really a forté

I'm going in directions decidedly
different

telling same stories in new ways

and this one

is about how Billy A

burned it down with YOU.

PART ONE

Introducing

Billy Aucaster

Bold

Brave

Bashful,

Billy Ancaster is one of those

not-particularly-good-at-
anything kind of protagonists,

though he fancies himself a
pugilist and a poet,

and so understanding the
particularly twisted kind of
psychology that produces either of
those professions is for your
particular consideration

--imagine the twisted fuck who
fancies himself both?

...

To make matters worse,

Billy Ancaster is aging the kind of
rapidly we collectively realize

just a little too late,

and so the road ahead

--a road filled with what he hopes
are the attentions of the beautiful
(always seemingly ortherwise-
committed) women

is maybe a little shorter in
distance
than the admittedly
impressive/horrifying

litter of hearts and corresponding
bodies

he left lying

on the road behind.

The Covid 19 pandemic,

now in Year Three

isn't helping

the not-so-quiet desperation

our Brave Billy is feeling,

and the most recent rebuking
of his most recent love,

and the immediately following and
equally awful

rebuking of the one right after,

have left Billy despondent and

maybe a little pissed,

and at the every-other girl

foolish enough to become
emotionally entangled with him

victims of the poetry on every page

that follows this one.

Let me tell you a little about

BILLY FUCKING ANCASTER

Billy Ancaster has a hole in his head.
(It's real, and it's on the cover of this
book.)

It's shaped like a heart, which is both fun
and maybe a little accurate,

because maybe there's a hole in his heart,
too.

And so one is frighteningly real
(--and not just because I'm really Billy
and that hole is really fucking scary)

and one is at least metaphorically real

and both matter because

both inform

the mistakes I made about you,

and the reason Billy

gets a book about him.

Billy

has a brother named **Johnny**

and Johnny Ancaster is a big part of this book.

Johnny Ancaster has a bit of a temper,

so keep that in mind,

but Johnny cares about his brother

--and is full of semi-well-intentioned good advice

so Billy takes his advice
in ways he really maybe only sometimes should.

Because Johnny is basically a pitbull
some deity shaved and pretended to pass as human

and so his worldview is restricted to
the kinds of things pitbulls pretending as
humans can't pretend to care about

chasing tail and eating raw and not
suffering fools or lesser canines

--things to keep in mind when considering
the perspectives supplied by

Johnny Fucking Ancaster.

A LITTLE MORE ABOUT BILLY A.

BILLY WAS BORN IN THE MUD AND THE
SUMMER

AND BOTH ARE REASONS

BILLY GETS A BOOK.

BECAUSE THE MUD MADE HIM ANGRY,

COMING THE WAY HE DID AND FROM
ABSOLUTELY NOTHING MORE.

AND THE SUMMER MADE HIM SELFISH,

ASTROLOGY CROWNING HIM LION AND
THEREFORE KING.

SO BILLY WAS A MESS

LONG BEFORE THE LOOKS
-HE WILL SO HUMBLY POINT OUT-

THAT LET HIM GET AWAY WITH IT,

ANGRY AND SELFISH AND UNLEASHED

UPON PRETTY GIRLS WHO SHOULD HAVE KNOWN
BETTER,

PRETTY GIRLS JUST LIKE

YOU.

nature **VS** nurture

...and it wasn't even close.

(brave)

BILLY ANCASTER &

The Thing About Fridays.

Billy Ancaster spends his Friday nights

getting punched in the face

hard,

because Billy Ancaster fashions himself a
boxer,

and because boxers do nothing if not box.

So Fridays end bloody

and Fridays end bruised

because the guy Billy boxes

is named Tyson (-really!)

and Ten-Round Tyson's got fifty pounds
on Billy easy,

and so Friday Night Fights are anything
but,

Billy working out as-advertised and
constantly-surfacing demons

hoping repeated head trauma

quiets the more restless

of voices whispering

in still-ringing ears.

JOHNNY ANCASTER

loves weed

like BILLY ANCASTER

loves unavailable women. *

So lots,

and the rest of this book

is about the litany of mistakes
made

under the influence

&

in service of

addictions both chosen

and wonderfully unavoidable.

Unavailable woman *

Careful putting prettily
manicured fingers through
proverbial and poorly-tethered
cages.

Late nights

are

for whiskey

and

fever dreams

and

the everything else I do

to fail at forgetting

you.

Billy Ancaster

is at the age

where life starts taking

the pop on his jab

his Aunt Lou

his first and favorite dog

and you

and you

and you

and you

and you

latest and last of the ones smart

enough to leave him

while he was good looking enough

to get away with it.

PART TWO

Big Red.

BIG RED
IS ANYTHING BUT,

ALL OF ONE HUNDRED AND
FIVE POUNDS

OF THE KIND OF PRETTY

THAT MAKES HER

A BIG FUCKING DEAL

FOR BOTH BILLY ANCASTER
AND THE REST OF THIS BOOK

BECAUSE HER UP AND LEAVING
HIM

AFTER THREE-AND-A-HALF
OF THE BEST YEARS OF HIS
LIFE

HAS LEFT HIM

ON THE KIND OF RAMPAGE

THAT WILL HAVE ALL OF THE
GIRLS

AFTER BIG RED

READING THIS BETWEEN THE
FINGERS

COVERING THEIR PRETTY-AS-WELL
EYES

AND NO LONGER WONDERING

JUST WHAT IN THE HELL

GOT INTO HIM

TO MAKE BRAVE BILLY ANCASTER

TAKE IT OUT ON EACH AND EVERY
ALL OF THEM

HOW WE GOT IN THIS MESS

BRAVE BILLY ANCASTER COMES HOME
BRAVELY
SOME MONDAY NIGHT AFTER WORK.

IT'S LATE, BECAUSE WORK GOES LATE—LATE
ENOUGH TO BE DARK OUTSIDE, DARK ON SOME
LATE SUMMER DAY.

BRAVE BILLY COMES HOME, AND—MAYBE ODE
TO HIS FORTHCOMING MISFORTUNE—
DOESN'T NOTICE IT'S UNUSUALLY DARK IN
HIS APARTMENT, AS WELL.

THERE'S A GIRL ON HIS ADMITTEDLY
EXPENSIVE COUCH,
WHICH ISN'T UNUSUAL,
TONIGHT (OR ANY OTHER, TO BE FAIR TO THE
APPEAL OF BRAVE BILLY)
AND IT'S NOT UNUSUAL TONIGHT,
BECAUSE

THE GIRL IS BIG RED,
AND BIG RED IS HIS GIRLFRIEND.

BIG RED IS SITTING IN THE DARK
AND BEFORE THE FIRST FLICK OF THE LIGHT
SWITCH
BRAVE BILLY CAN'T HELP BUT NOTICE
HOW HER EYES SEEM TO BE GLOWING,

GLOWING A LOT LIKE A RACCOON'S EYES SEEM
TO GLOW, RIGHT AFTER GETTING CAUGHT
WITH THEIR CUTE LITTLE PAWS GOING
THROUGH YOUR GARBAGE.

BRAVE BILLY FLICKS THE LIGHT SWITCH,
AND—QUICKER THAN THE ROOM CAN LIGHT
UP—BEGINS REGALING BIG RED WITH BIG
USELESS RECOUNTINGS OF THE COMPLETELY
MEANINGLESS EVENTS OF HIS BIG
INCONSEQUENTIAL DAY.

BRAVE BILLY FAILS TO NOTICE,
SOMEWHAT TRAGICALLY,
THAT THE WILD IN BIG RED'S EYES
HASN'T DISSIPATED WITH THE LIGHTING OF
THE ROOM AROUND HER.

NOW
BIG RED
IS REALLY LITTLE LILI,
BECAUSE THAT'S REALLY HER REAL NAME

BUT REGARDLESS OF WHAT HE CHOOSES TO
CALL HER, LITTLE LILI LISTENS POLITELY

THE WAY SHE HAS LISTENED POLITELY
TO THE RANTINGS OF BRAVE BILLY
FOR ALMOST FOUR YEARS.

WHEN HE'S DONE,
DONE WAILING ABOUT THE INCONSEQUENTIAL
EVENTS OF HIS INCONSEQUENTIAL DAY,
SHE POLITELY PARTS THE LIPS

ON HER PRETTY LITTLE FACE

AND TELLS HIM

IN EQUALLY PRETTY TONES AND WITH
MODESTLY CHOSEN WORDS

THAT SHE'S LEAVING HIM

IMMEDIATELY

AND TO MOVE THOUSANDS AND THOUSANDS OF
MILES

AWAY.

HE CAN'T COME
AND
SHE'S QUIT THE JOB
SHE HAD WORKING
AT THE SAME PLACE
AS BRAVE BILLY
ALREADY

AND

WHILE SHE WOULD VERY MUCH LIKE
TO LIVE WITH POOR BRAVE BILLY
FOR THE TWO WEEKS IT WILL TAKE

FOR HER TO BE READY TO UP AND LEAVE HIM,
FOR REAL,

SHE WOULD CERTAINLY UNDERSTAND
IF SHE COULD NOT.

HE LETS HER,
STAY

BECAUSE HE LOVES HER

AND WHEN THE TWO WEEKS ARE
UNMERCIFULLY
GONE

SO IS SHE,
BIG RED
OR
LITTLE LILI

LEAVES HIM
TO THE PROBABLY-BETTER LIFE
SOMEWHERE OUT WEST
HE JUST WASN'T LOVED ENOUGH
TO BE BROUGHT TO, TOO.
...

*PLUS, SHE LEAVES HIM IN THE MIDDLE OF A
PANDEMIC.

NO WONDER EVERYONE ELSE IN THIS BOOK IS FUCKED.

I'd say
I put my heart in it

but we both know
you took that

like that mug you know I loved,

cold comforts and coffee
all I'm left with

and the lack of warmth
heart
and
caffeinated thoughts

make Quarantine Confessions 3

your fault
and for more than
the oh-so-painfully obvious.

...

SO THERE YOU HAVE IT.

BRAVE BILLY ANCASTER

SPENDS THE REST OF THIS BOOK

GETTING PUNCHED IN HIS STUPID PRETTY
FACE,

AND NOW YOU KNOW WHY.

...

Big Red is gone
and he misses her,

and he takes her leaving

like a left from Ten-Round Tyson

first crack

in an already

slowly-cracking skull.

...

BIG RED REACHES OUT
FROM THE TOP OF
THE FUCKING MOUNTAIN
(LITERALLY)
HE MADE HER RUN AWAY
TO,
AND IN THE REACHING
REMINDS BRAVE BILLY
HOW MUCH OF HIMSELF
WAS LOST
ON THE DAY SHE
DROVE DIRECTIONS
PROMISING BEAUTIFUL VIEWS
AND
ANYTHING OTHER
THAN
FOOLISHLY PHONY
BRAVE LITTLE BOYS.

She says

"You're mine Billy Ancaster"

and it hurts

because it's true

and it hurts

because it took her

moving 2,000 miles

away

to stake a claim

she never had to.

BIG RED
's got someone ghostwriting her DM's
but Brave Billy isn't scared

he's been on some medium shit
seeing ghosts
since way back in '84

See, his chest Stays-Puft
Not the Marshmallow Man she figured
when she pulled the latest
scheme
on her steady-scheming shit.

*It might be the repeated blows to the
head

that make bold Billy question
the admittedly-questionably typed
messages from Big Red/Little Lili,

but

synapses both firing and missing

have him missing her

and rationalizing leavings

as betrayls

because

it's all he understands,

and because

it's the only language he speaks.

...

Billy goes bad
is the next part of this book,

somewhat logically...

...because bad things happen to Billy
and
as the back of this book will tell you,

Billy is just a sad, scared little boy.

So when bad things happen to
bad Billy,

you can bet your bottom dollar

bad things happen to
everyone around him

because, and maybe just.

PART THREE

Doomed.

This is the first
of the ones about
the one right after,

the rest of which
make about as much sense

as both her eyes
and their attempts at
something supposedly close to
courtship,

rest assured
our Brave Billy
burns it down

with this one
the way he tends to,

concussions and consternations

about all he's good for

and about all he's got left.

...

Same animals

bare teeth

never

bow heads

It starts slow,
this next thing
& on the heels of the last multi-year
disappointment,

like maybe her
up & leaving
left Billy Ancaster the kind of
vulnerable
that allowed you
to go from casual possibility
to doomed eventuality.

So it starts slow,
all selfies and all-the-time-
conversation,
picking up steam and
not so slowly
hurtling towards the eventuality that
will see
you
up and leave
Billy Ancaster,
too.

...

forward

I'm told these conversations are best
when waged with carefully chosen and
clearly-stated words;

and I'm sorry

but we both know

I prefer riddles and intentions relegated
just under surfaces

better unsurfaced

when it comes to aggressive eye contact
and the words you want to follow

I'd argue don't need to

and you'd argue

that arguing is more of what
these pretense-laden
conversations
inevitably descend to

because for a guy supposedly good
with words

when it comes to bravery in the face
of

that pretty fucking face of yours

I'm two left feet and left without
the words it would take

to converse civilly and convince
you otherwise.

Billy Ancaster

lost his mind mid-September.

He'd known her for years,

this reason for mid-September
madness,

all perpetually blue eyes

and the kind of body that
complimented her pretty in ways
that boys like Billy Ancaster
almost always fall for.

He'd known her for years,

but mid-September is when she
engaged in the kind of
conversations that only ever end
one way,

when it comes to Billy A.

She said she wasn't happy in her
marriage

said so without expressly saying so

words sweet like the whatever-the-
fuck she sipped on,

sitting on his expensive couch and sipping her expensive coffee and telling him the kinds of things she told him that first time she came over.

That first time would be the last time, but Billy couldn't possibly have known that, looking into her perpetually blue/green eyes and getting himself the in-over-his-head he tends to,

sometime just before this conversation ended in his bed.

...

But first,
energy.

THESE STORIES
DON'T END PRETTY

AND I LOSE EVERY FIGHT
I'VE EVER FOUGHT

BUT YOUR EYES DON'T MAKE SENSE

AND MY WILLINGNESS TO PICK MYSELF
UP OFF THE CANVAS
YOU PUT ME ON

MIGHT NOT EITHER,

BUT YOU'RE WORTH
AT LEAST TEN ROUNDS
AND THE HIT
BOTH MY RECORD AND
MY INFINITELY FRAGILE EGO

ARE ABOUT TO TAKE.

SO I GUESS WHAT
I'M SAYING IS

COME ON

TAKE WHAT YOU WANT

WHAT'S ONE MORE BUSTED LIP

TO A BARELY TETHERED HEART.

....

Best guess
she broke him
that first time she came over,

sometime between his rubbing her low
back on the balcony
and
the feeling he felt the first time she
rested her weary head on his chest.

She would regress
immediately after,

well, sometime between her drive home
and
whatever happened with her husband when
she got there,

but by the time he noticed
his heart was in it

the way his heart hadn't been in it
since Big Red.

Billy hated regression
the way Billy kinda hated everything
the morning after she was gone,

and that was before
he realized that
for good
was the kind of gone
she really was

maybe moments after he let her drive
home.

The concussions
--more accurately, the
trauma

have one beautiful benefit
for forlorn Billy Ancaster

--he only remembers
the good
band-aids the bad
and can't help but wonder
why she
takes her time
before responding
to his always ill-timed and worse-taken
invitations into
the vacuum that is
his orbit.

Your neck of the woods
because you're not local
but
you're not available, either
and that's never stopped us before.

And you can blame
your oft-referenced crippling anxiety
for reasons you won't
come out of the house
you supposedly no longer share

I'm here and waiting
maybe less than patiently
for you to realize
isolation
is better spent
anywhere but the

alone

you're so intent on imposing.

She struggles
and with more than her mental
and for far longer
than Bold Billy
and his
"let me fuck with your mental"
leanings,

so when she
doesn't look at him
with eyes that don't make sense

--and because she lives too far away to
come over

telling him

"I want to work on my marriage, I hope you
understand"

he handles it
about as well as you'd imagine
and he

begins to unravel
at seams that were really never raveled

understanding nothing
despite assurances otherwise

and although
her marriage
is the kind of over
she was last weekend,

we all know
Bold Billy

won't hang around patiently
to pick up

the inevitable pretty pieces.

ALL DUE RESPECT
BUT

I KNEW YOU FIRST

AND
I LIKE(d) YOU MORE.

LOYALTY B(L)INDS.

He falls in love with the next one
well before he has any right to,

maybe because he loves her
maybe because he loves *her*

and either way
because
the whole wide world can't burn fast
enough

to make up for the hurt they've
collectively caused him.

Brash Billy Ancaster
good out the gate,
not so good
at the gates/cages
being good out of
eventually find him
painfully/terribly
trapped in.

SHE'S PULLING AWAY
AND
IN SO DOING
WINNING THE PROVERBIAL FIGHT
EVERY SINGLE ENTANGLEMENT
SORT OF IS,

AND
IF THERE'S ONE THING BILLY ANCASTER
HATES
IT'S LOSING ROUNDS

TO OPPOSITION HE'S CONFIDENT HE CAN
HANDLE

AND
HE CAN'T
HANDLE
ANYTHING REMOTELY RESEMBLING
THE REGRESSION

SHE'S SET ON REGRESSING TO,
THROWING WORDS

AND
WITH LESS FREQUENCY
THAN HE'S USED TO

AND
HE'S FRUSTRATED AND MOST LIKELY
CONCUSSED

AND SO
IT'S

A MESSAGE TO HER
IN THE DARK AND DESPERATION
AND THROWING THE ONE WORD

NO SELF-RESPECTING ROMEO
EVERY REALLY SHOULD.

Brave Billy
insofar as
he says the words
eyes do
but
pretty lips
won't painfully
part to.

NOTHING HURTS

LIKE WELL-TIMED LEFT HOOKS

AND

HEARING "NO THANK YOU"

IN RESPONSE TO
POORLY-TIMED

"I LOVE YOUS"

-billy ancaster.

*didn't mention that

poorly-timed "I love yous" were really
confused feelings

masquerading as Hail Marys

for the head trauma-induced

and really poorly-timed words

that led to the need for Hail Marys, at
all.

Twisting tongues and feelings

trying to rationalize

situations that are anything but.

"I LOVE YOU"

is a mistake

always, and especially first

first signal
that you're waving white flags

and signaling
the loss of the only war
even remotely worth
fighting

the jockeying for
position, pole
in the battle to

at once

lose yourself and retain
that last little piece of
the dignity a

clearly spoken

"I LOVE YOU"

proves you maybe never had

if not most certainly just lost.

It was your eyes
that got us into this
mess,
but I can't fault you
for that.

It's my
fault
maybe calling you mine
before I had anything
remotely
close to the right to

and I was wrong
but not about the
wanting you
the way I really,
really
wanted you,

No
I was wrong
for maybe believing a
guy like me
deserved anything close
to
the way those eyes fell
on me
hoping maybe you'd
fall.

too.

Mr. Melancholy.

no offense, but the opp

(--and I don't mean your husband)

looks about five-six

and the kind of gassed-up

that makes making my age

the impossibility

we're turning out to be.

_____ aka

"Doomed"

is gone
and he misses her,

and he takes her leaving

like another left from Ten-Round Tyson

latest crack

coming decidedly close to

the last crack,

too many

too soon

for a

not so slowly-cracking skull.

...

BROKEN BILLY ANCASTER
CAN'T HELP BUT WONDER

WHAT'S WITH THESE BITCHES
UP AND DRIVING AWAY ON HIM

all these

months

and all these miles

and the bitch of it is

we both know I'm

still

simply ten digits and

one full tank away.

get over it

the tiny voice in the back of his still-
aching head said,

but the tiny voice is the same
one that told him
and on more than one occasion

don't get punched in the face
don't listen to Johnny Ancaster
let that kick in the balls from Johnny
Reimer go, it was twenty-nine years ago

and he hadn't bothered
with any of that

so the odds
of bold Billy Ancaster
getting over you

are about as likely
as the listening to reason
he hasn't done/won't do
since the tiny voice in the back of his
pretty-much-always aching head

suggested the first of the
semi-well-intentioned good ideas
long before the balls that would
inevitably be kicked

dropped

far too many better-yet-not-ignored
impulses ago.

...

IYKYK

Miss more
than your eyes
and that ass

and you blame me for
books written about both

but neither make sense

—what about us does tho

all false starts and fumbles
gnashed teeth and
terrible and terribly misinterpreted
words

trying to find
ways to say
words we really don't need to

words like

miss

and more than
the things we've established

I really do.

"You're not who I thought you were"

well,
You're not who I thought you were, either
and
your poorly disguised/easily translated
subtle little selfies
don't hit the same
and
you can blame the lighting
or the lack of open gyms,

either way
me and Drake will be over here
getting over you not so quietly
all Marvin's Room cranked on speakers
next to couches
I barely remember you curling up on.

...

Blame the
nothing-we-can-do-about-it
hole

in Brave Billy's
beautiful little head,

but the fucks he used to give
are decidedly less,

and so he's coming
quite frankly
for anyone who's hurt him
and the list is long
and his way with words hasn't waned
the way his memory
is trying to,

and so Quarantine Confessions 3
is The Ballad of Billy Ancaster
and a race to
remember
everyone who needs appropriate
rememberings

here on the path of his
war waged for revenge.

Poor
Billy Ancaster
lost his mind mid-September
broke his nose sometime after
broke his heart
a little too close
to the losing of things
that preceded the
swiftly transpiring
& ultimately inevitable
slew of breakings.

PART FOUR

Johnny Fucking Ancaster.

Johnny Ancaster

is into the weed again.

The weed & his feelings,

if and only because the two are anything
but mutually exclusive.

And you'd be surprised to learn that
shaved-down, pass-as-human pitbulls

feel things like feelings,

but Johnny Ancaster

is into the weed again,

and so here come the first of many
insightful and longing-fueled feelings.

"You know"
says Johnny Ancaster
"the trouble with the women we tend to
attract/fall for"

before continuing & between hits of
rapidly disappearing blunts

Johnny Ancaster pauses for dramatic
effect

if and only because Johnny Ancaster is
nothing if not

a little dramatic.

"The trouble with the women"

--and I'll spare you the rest,
because the rest

is what the rest

of this whole goddamn book

is all about.

...

Getting involved
with an Ancaster
is equivalent
--more or less
--to
mainlining heroin
and sitting
through
Sunday service
at your local
place of worship

like the good
is really good
but kinda comes nowhere close
to scrubbing
the sins
it took
to sit that pretty ass
in that fucking pew.

...

So

BILLY ANCASTER

tells JOHNNY ANCASTER

he's in love,

and this one's different

(and not just because Johnny Ancaster
never hears Billy Ancaster use words like
the words he just used)

and this one's complicated

(and not just because this one is married)

(--to be fair, they're all married)

no, this one's different

because the look in Billy Ancaster's little lady-killing eyes

says so without the saying so

his little lady-killing lips move

to subsequently say so.

So,

Johnny Ancaster

tells Billy Ancaster

he's a fucking idiot

(and not just because he fucking is)

he tells him

because he's hoping his words aren't wasted

on still-ringing ears,

head-trauma or energy-induced

lovings aside.

Words of wisdom are always absorbed,

if not appreciated

for offering fair warnings.

...

Johnny Ancaster
has a bit of a cough, tonight

and while that's not unusual
 considering
the copious amounts of weed
he's typically consuming,

the cough tonight isn't typical
--and this isn't the book for subtle
foreshadowing,
so turn the page
and enjoy a not-so-subtle reminder
the world we're in
is still fucked
and far harder
than even your most earnest
Ancaster
ever could.

JOHNNY FUCKING ANCASTER
IS VIOLENTLY ILL
AND HE SWEARS IT'S NOT COVID
WHEN IT CLEARLY FUCKING IS.

AND HE'S BEING
A LITTLE STUBBORN AND STUPID,
IF AND ONLY BECAUSE
STUBBORN AND STUPID
ARE TWO THINGS ANCASTERS DO
VERY VERY WELL.

BEING SICK,
NOT SO MUCH

AND SO IT'S DAYS WORTH OF
COLD SWEATS
AND HOT SOUPS,

REFLECTING ON THE CHOICES
THAT LED HIM HERE,
LYING IN A SHEET-SOAKED BED
AND WONDERING
IF MAYBE THERE'S SOMETHING TO
THIS IMAGINARY PANDEMIC-THING
AFTER ALL.

Johnny Ancaster
might be the first
person in the country
to have Flurona,

he's that sick
and sick of
this latest lockdown
he's found himself in
bed and maybe sleeping
through,
and when he's awake
he's calling with
profound meditations
as to why

both Billy and Johnny
Ancaster
tend to pandemic
alone,
no one to care for them
when unforeseen
variants
up and overcome them.

"We need to do things
a little different"

proclaims **Johnny Ancaster**

boldy and from

the not-so-sanct sanctity

of his COVID-maybe deathbed.

Having made the first of many

bold proclamations

after realizing that

maybe living forever

isn't in the cards

the way near-death escapes

--and previously not-really-caring

if near-death escapes

were near or not at all--

have left him

both lying and thinking.

So he is,

Johnny Ancaster

both lying and thinking

and about the way they view the world

and all of the beautiful women

within it;

like maybe there's more

than selfishly motivated conquest

to courting

the fairer of the sexes

and for more than just sex

--like maybe there's something to

having someone there

to care

in ways that brothers just can't

when the proverbial chips are down

and this made up sickness

is making people

really fucking sick.

Johnny Ancaster
is on the mend
and from the Flurona
that more than likely
tried to kill him,

his furious anger
and the metabolic function that follows
more than likely
his sole saving grace.

Regardless,
Johnny Ancaster is back
and realizing
his lust for life
and the women that run/ruin his
deserve at least equally-angered
attentions

to the attentions he so attentively paid
them, collectively, before

the 'Rona tried to kill him.

So he's back,
Johnny Ancaster
and on the blunts
and no longer blunting
the more taciturn
of the tone he uses
when he picks up the phone to call them,

making up for both
lost time and
the lack of drama said lost time
must have mercifully allowed them.

Johnny Ancaster
has been in touch with a number of them,

women

and from his past,

and one, in particular,
takes an interest in
his recovery

reconnecting
over
shared calamities,

because as it turns out
she's recovering, too.

So the first Friday
he's on his feet and able

he's hosting
Lizzy-Come-Lately,

a former lover
and

one who always had
that particular kind of patience

needed for guys like him.

So

JOHNNY ANCASTER

tells BILLY ANCASTER

he's in love,

and this one's different

(and not just because Billy Ancaster never hears Johnny Ancaster use words like the words he just used)

and this one's complicated

(and not just because this one is back, and off the blocked-for-the-better-part-of-the-last-year list)

no, this one's different

because the look in Johnny Ancaster's
little pitbull-looking eyes

says so without the saying so

his puffy little pitbull lips move

to subsequently say so.

So,

Billy Ancaster

tells Johnny Ancaster

he's a fucking idiot

(and not just because he fucking is)

he tells him

because he's hoping his words aren't
wasted, and not just because this is
turning out to be somewhat of a previously
uncharacteristic pattern with the
Ancaster brothers

but because brothers are nothing

if not overly concerned for one another.

So Johnny takes the advice,

but not quite as good as he gives it,

absorbing more than just weed smoke when
Billy tells Johnny he loves him

because he's man enough to admit it

and he hopes it works out for him

because he really hopes it does.

...

It turns out
Lizzy-Come-Lately
is good for
Johnny Fucking Ancaster.

I mean, they fight
but fighting with Johnny Fucking
Ancaster
is just what people do.

Between impassioned battlings
and bi-weekly breakups
that always seemingly result in
bi-weekly make-ups

they spend almost every waking minute
attached to the weekends she drives down
in

doing the kinds of things
people connecting post-Covid
tend to do,

so lots of being places
and doing things
and enjoying the company
old flings and new perspectives

tend to provide.

Which is fine by brash Billy

because he's left
with more time to take out recent
hurtings
on Other Married Women

doing the kinds of things
that really shouldn't have him wondering

how he ends up the alone
this book has already
spent pages in
the foretelling.

PART FIVE

The Other Married Women

Billy Ancaster fucks them

like he hates them.

And the irony is

he doesn't hate them at all.

Quite the opposite

though the hatred isn't internal
either

(--because, as Billy Ancaster will
attest, no one will or could ever
love Billy Ancaster as much as
Billy Ancaster loves Billy
Ancaster)

he fucks them

like he hates where he comes from

and he fucks them

like he hates where he's going

and like he hates where this night
is going

five seconds after

said fucking is done.

"What's this one

about?"

...

Blowjobs

&

Boxing.

HIM IN THE RING HER IN THE BED

HE TAKES IT OUT ON EACH EQUALLY

EXPRESSING EXTERNALLY
WARS ORIGINATING OPPOSITE

AND OPPOSING ALMOST EVERYTHING
THAT MAKES THE MISTAKE

OF CROSSING HIM

RIGHT CROSSES,

OR WRONG GAZES.

Married women
do it better

and their
husbands won't
tell you so

because their
husbands aren't
the ones getting
fucked.

*actually, wait.

They are
getting fucked.

Just in non-
sexual, 'do-it-
better, what's-
that?'

ways.

He goes for those

otherwise committed

maybe because

committed

is about the only word he

does not believe in

The other married women matter

just maybe not enough
for their very own section
in this very book.

This very book
would be way too big,
honestly if not modestly,

if he had secrets for, say

HER

the one who took his heart
and his hometown
way before
it was fashionable
for the pain needed to fashion
books like this one.

There are books about her,
and
to be honest,
part of every book hereafter
will have a little part of her in it,

but by this book,
she's the kind of married
that means

while she loves him
very very much

she's more than likely

never coming back

*winky face emoji

because she might,
but not by the time
this book comes out

and so this book
is about the messes he's made
since she took up and
took his hometown.

...

Who could forget about

Her

married—and to Jesus (!)

which told bold Billy Ancaster
she was a sinner

well before she fucked around
and really proved it.

HE REMEMBERS
HER

FIRST OF THE MARRIED WOMEN
WHO WENT OFF AND HAD A KID OR TWO

AND THEN REMEMBERED
SHE LOVED BOLD BILLY

COMING BACK AFTER
ALL THESE YEARS

AND FUCKING AROUND
WITH
MORE THAN THE STABILITY
OF HER STABLE LITTLE HOUSEHOLD

FUCKING WITH
BOLD BILLY AND
FORGETTING WHY
SHE WAS SMART TO TRY AND STAY AWAY
ALL THOSE YEARS AGO

She

had a husband he knows
and knows quite well,

and he liked him, even

--he just liked her
a little bit more.

Her.

he had fun with
and her husband
was a nice enough
guy
he just
preferred
the closed-door
encounters
he found himself
encountering
on nights
attached to
the days
she should have
been at home with
him.

She

wanted to move from Arizona
so he called her AZ
anything but easy
with those big blue eyes
and the kind of
wild energy
that made her looking for homes
in towns adjacent to his
the kind of good idea
it probably really wasn't.

She was distractingly beautiful
and he loved her job and her voice and
might have maybe loved her, too

but his wild
mixed a little wrong with her wild

and so his international experiment
ended in the kind of tiny tragedy
all of the stories about women in these
pages
tend to.

Her

he called co-worker
and he never called her
but still she came over
and left her husband at
home

reinforcing with every
other headboard-rattling
thought of reinforcing his
headboard that
his previously ascertained
assertion that marriage,
like love,
is simply not to be either
had or trusted.

Thoughts of

Her

he would like to keep all to

himself

DM me
for a semi-serious
seriously-dangerous
&
only initially

good time.

PART SIX

Fighting

Ten Round Tyson.

Ten-round Tyson
looks a little like Billy,
and I'm talking before the
matching black eyes
and bloody noses.

He could be
the Third Ancaster Brother
and he fights like it too,

beating brave Billy
like big brothers
almost always
beat brothers, smaller.

So it's not like there is
no love there,
beatings administered
on both ends
with a begrudging mutual respect
usually reserved for

those who share blood
on more than
shared white towels.
...

BILLY ANCASTER
GETS HIS NOSE BROKEN
ROUND TWO
OF A TEN-ROUND FIGHT.

AND DESPITE COMMON SENSE
AND A DATE ON SUNDAY

HE TAKES TWENTY FOUR
MORE
MINUTES OF PUNCHES
TO HEAVILY-BLEEDING PARTS OF
FACES

FACING DOWN DEMONS

AND WHATEVER THE HELL ELSE

THESE VS TYSON FRIDAY-NIGHT
FIGHTS

HAVE STIRRED UP
IN BILLY ANCASTER

AND WELL BEFORE
BROKEN NOSES
AND SAID
BLEEDINGS.

...

IT WAS A LEFT HOOK
THAT PUNCHED A HOLE IN
BRAVE BILLY ANCASTER'S
PRETTY LITTLE HEAD.

A LEFT HOOK
OR LEFT HOOK, RIGHT CROSS
DAMNED IF BILLY CAN REMEMBER

THE WAY LEFT HOOKS HAVE LEFT BRAVE
BILLY

STRUGGLING TO REMEMBER VERY MUCH AT
ALL.

SO IT'S LESS ABOUT PUNCHES

AND MORE ABOUT REPERCUSSIONS

BECAUSE ALTHOUGH IT WOULD BE
CONVENIENT

CONCUSSIONS AND THE SUBSEQUENT RASH
DECISIONS

CONCUSSIONS TEND TO CAUSE

CAN'T BE FULLY BLAMED

FOR THE BAD DECISIONS UNFOLDING ON
EVERY PAGE

THAT FOLLOWS THIS ONE.

BEHOLD
BRAVE BILLY ANCASTER

ALL CROOKED NOSE
AND
CROOKED SMILE
AND
CHOCK-FUCKING FULL
OF
THE KINDS OF CROOKED DEEDS
SAID SMILE LET HIM GET AWAY
WITH
SOME PUNCHES BEFORE FORTY
AND THE KIND OF CROOKED
LEFT LEANING NOSES
AND RAPIDLY LEAVING WOMEN
SEEM TO HAVE LEFT HIM TO

REMINDING BRAVE BILLY
ANCASTER
IN MIRRORS BOTH REAL AND
IMAGINED
THAT NO ONE GETS AWAY
CLEAN,

LEAST OF ALL
POOR
BRAVE BILLY ANCASTER.

Head trauma
is only in the movies

brave Billy Ancaster tells himself

in between the bleeding
he's currently bleeding
post-boxing
and on white towels
that quite frankly can't take it.

And maybe it amuses him,
the thought of white towels
throwing in the proverbial towel

signaling the end of fights
they can no longer take,

white towels
increasingly pink

when they emerge from super-necessary
washes

on next mornings he feels
increasingly dizzy awakening in.

...

Want to quit

with every blank page
so you're welcome
for two-hundred-something
tiny testaments
to my stubbornness.

WANT TO QUIT

EVERY TIME HE STEPS THROUGH THE
ROPES

BUT TEN ROUNDS
AND
TWENTY BRUISES AFTER

HE'S REASONABLY SURE HE MADE
THE RIGHT DECISION.

maybe the mirror
fights back harder
than Ten-Round Tyson

(although the wounds still-and-barely
healing from Friday last scream loudly
in their collective begging to differ)

regardless,
Billy Ancaster

finds one
decidedly harder

to still-swollen
face these days.

...

HE FIGHTS
MORE THAN HE WRITES
THESE DAYS

AND MAYBE BECAUSE
THE LATTER
HITS HARDER
THAN THE FORMER

SURFACE LEVEL BRUISING
HEALS FASTER

AND THE BROKEN NOSE
AND THE CRACKED RIBS
AND THE HOLE IN HIS FUCKING SKULL

CUMULATIVELY
ARE OF LESSER CONCERN
THAN FACING DOWN

THE REASONS
THEY LEAVE HIM

AND TO THE
WRITING

HE LEAVES FOR THE NIGHTS
ATTACHED TO THE DAYS

HE CAN COME EVEN CLOSE
TO FACING THE REASONS WHY.

PART SEVEN

lockdown 4

BECAUSE BEHAVING IN A PANDEMIC
IS SOMETHING NO RESTLESS SOUL
SHOULD EVEN REMOTELY ATTEMPT TO DO.

The pharmacy is giving out booster shots
of various essential vaccines

and so Billy Ancaster takes
the jab
between scouring the coffee aisle
for coffee pods
and forgetting the first of
the essentials he'll inevitably
return for.

The booster shot
made everyone he knows
feel the kind of horrible
this prolonged pandemic
pretty much has them used to

but 10 round Billy
is in the ring
the very next night
trading punches
and theories
as to why
the punches, physical
hurt less and leave fewer marks
than the hits he's taken from
her
that drove him to tonight and
this ring
and
said feelings
to begin with.

Covid cases
go up in winter

because that's what
fucking Covid cases
do,

and while Billy Ancaster
is nothing if not brave,

he can't help but wonder
if he can take the hit on the chin

(proverbial or otherwise)

another rash of
rashly-decided upon government
lockdowns

will have upon a
psyche

black and blue
and marred from more than just

the repeated head trauma
and the repeated leavings
that maybe caused it.

So winter is dark
and more than metaphorically

and Billy waits
alone on the couch he once shared

for tidings that portent doom
this New Year less fun that the last.

THE GOVERNMENT
ANNOUNCED LOCKDOWN
NUMBER FOUR
TODAY,
AND IT'S FOUR TOO MANY
AND IT'S FAR TOO OFTEN
AND THE LAST THREE YEARS
HAVE LEFT THE BROTHERS
ANCASTER
DESPONDENT AND MAYBE
A LITTLE DEPRAVED,
AND
--AS EXCUSES GO--
IT'S NOT THE BEST

BUT IN LIEU OF THE REST
OF THE ADMITTEDLY
ATROCIOUS BEHAVIOR
IN THE PAGES BOTH BEFORE
AND AFTER THIS ONE,

IT WILL JUST HAVE TO DO.

...

THE LOCKDOWN
HAS LEFT HIM ALONE
TONIGHT

ALONE IN A LOCKDOWN
WHILE THE WOMEN HE
ENTERTAINS
AND ENTERTAIN HIM
ARE CUDDLED UP ON
COUCHES
LESS EXPENSIVE BUT
BETTER EQUIPPED
WITH PEOPLE TO
CUDDLE.

AND SO EACH AND
EVERY
ALL OF THEM
ARE UP ON THE
PROVERBIAL SEESAW

HE CLIMBED ON
MAYBE KNOWING
HE WOULD LOSE

CHILDHOOD GAMES
RESULTING IN
NOTHING MORE THAN
LONELY NIGHTS
ATOP UNCUDDLED AND
DECIDEDLY COLDER
COUCHES.

Billy Ancaster
tragically/inevitably
spends his holidays alone

self-imposed & externally obligated
isolations

do little for still-healing hearts,
while working wonders for
still-mending noses.

So Christmas hits harder
than the left hooks that left him here

lying in bed alone

and

maybe to himself when he

closes

still-swollen eyes and

pretends

it's anything remotely close

to okay.

...

THE PLACE I'M FROM
ISN'T A PLACE
AND
THE CITY I CLAIM
IS SO SICK
AND OF ALL OF THIS
AND NOT FROM THE PANDEMIC
BUT FROM THE HYSTERIA AND FAKE SHIT
THIS PANDEMIC REALLY WROUGHT
LESS SICKNESS
MORE PROPAGANDA

LIKE WHEN DO WE
COLLECTIVELY CLAIM
KEEP YOUR SUBSIDIES
WE'RE HEAVY ON SOME
SEMBLANCE OF NORMAL SHIT

Billy Ancaster
isn't so good
and woefully
equipped
to take the L's
passing days
are beginning to
impart.

PART EIGHT

Gypsy .

That gypsy
has a boyfriend

but
Billy Ancaster
doesn't care
and maybe that gypsy
likes Billy Ancaster
just enough to not care, too.

And so she's over, that gypsy
and on expensive couches and
in between sips of semi-expensive
gin

she makes the mistake
they all make
in surprisingly similar
circumstances,

assuming brave Billy Ancaster
is anything other than as-
advertised

on surfaces cleaner than
the well-worn leather
she rests

her well-appointed ass upon.

...

The gypsy
is beautiful
really,

and despite being
really really beautiful
she's not
the self-absorbed
the self-absorbed women
he tends to fall for
typically tend to be

she's sensitive
like him, and
although bold Billy Ancaster
would never admit such a thing
he's the most sensitive boy
in the whole wide world

and so
the gypsy
is his kind of girl, for reasons beyond
her very real beauty.

The gypsy
is otherwise committed,
which is really kind of his thing too,

so beyond
her big brown eyes
and her big brown boyfriend
bold Billy Ancaster
likes her for reasons
beyond the reasonable reasons
he typically tends to.

She spends time, mercifully
and unmercifully it's never enough
to satisfy the utterly unsatiable
needs of bold Billy,

forever alone and
always on the nights
she doesn't grace him
with her graceful presence.

He tells her he understands,
other commitments and all,
but the utterly unreasonable
little lion in him
roars every night
she's anywhere but
beside/atop him.

WE'RE IN TRAFFIC AND
YOU'RE NOT ON MY LAP
ONLY BECAUSE OF THE SIZE OF THE
CENTER CONSOLE
AND THE CORRESPONDING SIZE OF
YOUR BIG FAT ASS,

AND I'M NOTHING IF NOT
HERE FOR
THE PLACES YOUR HAND IS PROBING

WONDERING LESS
ABOUT HOW WE'LL GET OUT OF
THIS MOTHERFUCKING TRAFFIC JAM

AND
WONDERING MORE
ABOUT HOW WE'LL GET OUT OF
THE CIRCUMSTANCES SURROUNDING
THIS LITTLE TRIP WE'VE SNUCK OFF
TO HAVE TOGETHER

YOUR BOYFRIEND BACK HOME
EAGER TO MARRY YOU

AND
MAKE YOU THE 'UNAVAILABLE'
THE REST OF THE MARRIED WOMEN
I'M USED TO WASTING MY TIME ON

LEFT ME TO,
SO DON'T
LEAVE ME TOO

FOR NOW
STUCK WITH YOU

AND

FOR ONCE
GRATEFUL

FOR MOTHERFUCKING TRAFFIC.

...

SHE DRINKS GIN
WITH A PURPOSE

AND THAT PURPOSE
MIGHT JUST BE

FORGETTING THE REASONS
REAL AND ATTACHED TO DECIDEDLY LESS
COOL NAMES

THAT ALMOST PREVENTED
HER SHARING THIS COUCH

AND THIS GIN
WITH LITTLE OLD BILLY A.

He's been
drinking
her gypsy tears
since before
drinking
gypsy tears
was a thing.

*Actually, maybe it's better to say
he's been drinking her gypsy tears
long after
drinking gypsy tears was a thing

because drinking gypsy tears
seems like something
wild boys like him
did way back when.

**Either way, he drinks them,
and
in a laundry list of
really kinky things
he'd like to do with and to her,

drinking her tears
is by far the tamest.

SHE DRINKS GIN
LIKE MAYBE SOME SMALL PART OF HER
HATES THE WORLD
EVEN HALF AS MUCH
AS SHE QUIETLY UNDERSTANDS HE REALLY
DOES

STARING INTO HIS
STUPID BLACKENED EYES
AND MAYBE LOVING THE DANGER
IF NOT THE BOY

BECAUSE BILLY ANCASTER
COMES AS ADVERTISED
SCREAMING AT HER
WITH QUIET DESPERATION

SITTING THERE
AND NOT SCREAMING
ON THE COUCH HE WAITS FOR HER ATOP.

Her ass
is the kind
that's really just not,

hurting him
the way it does

looking at it
under the constricting fabric of those
jeans and
wondering

what it will take
bold Billy Ancaster
to uncover it

the way she
by the looks of her, lying ass up on the
other side of his frankly-ridiculously
expensive couch

really really wants him to

too.

SHE DRINKS GIN
FAST
BECAUSE SHE KNOWS SHE HAS TO GO

BEING HERE
WITH HIM
NOT THE PLACE SHE SUPPOSES SHE IS
SUPPOSED TO BE

SOMEBODY DECIDEDLY NOT HIM
WAITING BACK HOME

AND FOR HER TO COME

THE WAY BILLY ANCASTER
IS HOPING SHE COMES TOO

DIFFERENT SPELLING
DIFFERENT INTENTIONS

THE DECIDEDLY DARKER OF WHICH
HAVE AN INCREASINGLY OFTEN HABIT

OF KEEPING HER
HERE.

Her ass
doesn't make sense

and her eyes aren't so bad
either

big and brown
and looking at him

the way they have been, off and on
and for the better part of eight years

the wonderings behind them
likely related to

thoughts of why
supposedly brave Billy Ancaster

is taking so fucking long
to come out and tell her

the things about her
aside from her no-sense ass

he has come to appreciate.

The gypsy comes over
for the hat she pretends she
left here,
brave Billy's apartment
on a Tuesday afternoon
they both really should be
somewhere decidedly else.

They wrestle,
verbally
with the things they often
non-verbally
wrestle with,

frustration and energy and
contemplated and increasingly
surfacing vulnerabilities

surfacing
between sips of the Gin she's
come to expect
on the somehow always sunny
Tuesday afternoons
she spends her should-be-
somewhere-elses

with today-bashful Billy.

Twisting arms
metaphorically
for my one hour a week

twisting arms
literally
trying to get you to stay
past pre-determined and already
allocated times

and

he calls more than he should
on moments you're away
and from him
and the seemingly oppressive
amount of time he so seemingly requires

time you begrudgingly acknowledge
is better spent with
me
twisting arms and otherwise
intertwined
atop couches
and
only because
you remain a little too good-girl
for more than subtly-suggested
bed alternatives.

Monday night
mid-pandemic
and he waits for her
to come over
or
maybe at least call

--it's not like they had concrete plans,
what with her having a particularly
needy boyfriend, and all

but tentative plans are the closest he
gets anyways,
and she is
nothing if not (*surprisingly) tentative
even after all these years
of him being the (*only) other guy,

and so his Monday ends
the kind of disappointing
Monday nights
mid-pandemic
unsurprisingly and yet still
disappointingly

almost always end.

...

She says he's taking her down South
somewhere
and
the somewhere is where he comes from
and
the why is some really poorly kept secret
about how we plans to marry her

or
at the very least, begin the process
with the presentation of some ring, or
something

--listening to her,
there on the couch they cuddle on,
bold Billy can't be bothered
with wonderings and as to the ceremonies
attached
to silly circumstances he doesn't
understand

and
he believes her,
the way he always believes her

but some small part of him wonders

--of all the fights he's always fighting
this is probably the one
and for her
and for his place in her life

he really probably should.

He lets her leave,

couches and countries, bound for
somewhere South and so obviously better,

because when it comes to fighting for
the things he deserves
that aren't attached to brain-damaging
beatings

brave Billy

really isn't that brave,

after all.

...

You're The Only One I
Can Talk To

on some

You're The Only One I
Can Talk to

shit,

and the _ _ _ _ty thing
of it is,

we can't talk anymore

your need to

go off and get married

to some guy who isn't
me

leaves The Only
Therapy I Know

to empty couches
and really good DVSN
songs.

*Do It Well, DVSN. Go listen to that shit.

You're gin
she's whiskey
(big fan of both)
one burns a little more
one presents a little sweet
both
slowly kill the same.

the gypsy is gone
and he misses her,

and he takes her leaving

like the last left from Ten-Round Tyson

he can possibly take,

last crack

in an already

completely cracked skull.

...

PART NINE

non

denominational

Yearnings

Balenciaga bags are cool and all

--but have you tried not pissing them off
in the first place?

(*apologies are increasingly expensive.)

WE BOTH KNOW I LIED

WHEN I SAID I DIDN'T LIKE
THAT TAYLOR SWIFT SONG.

We're here because we believed the things we told ourselves about each other.

. . .

I'M NOT WHO YOU COME HOME TO
WHEN YOU WANT HAPPY OR FULFILLED
OR FOREVER

OR ANY OF THE OTHER THINGS
A MAN WITH THE QUALITIES I
CLEARLY LACK
CAN GIVE YOU

NO,

I'M WHO YOU COME TO
WHEN YOU'RE SAD
AND YOU'RE LONELY

AND YOU'RE FEELING ALL OF THE
FEELINGS
WE BOTH KNOW I'VE GOT PLENTY OF

PLENTY OF,

AND MORE THAN HAPPY TO SHARE.

I DON'T CARE WHERE

JUST FAR

CHINO USED TO SING
BACK WHEN ANGST WAS JUST SOMETHING
PEOPLE OLDER THAN

YOUNG BILLY ANCASTER

SANG ABOUT ON
THE SAD SONGS
HE SOMEHOW ALWAYS KNEW
WOULD END UP BEING
ALL ABOUT HIM.

Is there anything better
in this whole wide world
coffee after whiskey
after
aching after you.

She's dry humping him
on his really expensive couch,
but all Billy Ancaster can think about
is the leaving
that's the last thing
on her horny little mind.

And so this one
is more about where his goes,
mind on matters other than
the admittedly important matter
mattering atop him right now.

It's insight, maybe
that mid-grind reminder that
the reader in you might maybe appreciate,
like maybe there's more to
our brave Billy Ancasater
than receiving admittedly-attention-
worthy grindings

from the enthusiastic if otherwise
committed
women,

women like the woman
enthusiastically demanding the totality
of his attentions
from her position atop astonishingly,
(*really!) expensive couches.

Tell me something
sweet,
it's been a bad
year
—or two
—or three
and
this badly
breaking heart
can't take
the more direct
of your break—my
—heart

breaking my
heart
words.

Needed You then

not so much now

someday in the not so distant

future

his tombstone reads

HERE LIES

brave

BILLY ANCASTER

he never got over it

Call me
DaddyWordsSoGood

Quasi Over It.

The Weeknd came early
like Abel dropped on Thursday
and bold Billy Ancaster awaits
the inevitable arrival of the DMs
that will determine the direction
not even Thursday debauchery
will most certainly take him

●●●

Equal parts out to getcha
and terrified you'll really get me.

IT'S LATE
BECAUSE THAT'S WHEN THE WRITING COMES
AND
EASIER AFTER THAT SECOND GLASS
OF SOMETHING STRONG
AND ENOUGH
TO MAKE THE MIND SETTLE
ON
SOMETHING WORTH SETTLING ON

SCRATCHING AT BOTH
OLD WOUNDS
AND THE MOON
AND WONDERING
WHY I PICKED UP THE PEN
TO BOTHER WITH ANY
OF THE WONDERINGS
A STILL WANDERING MIND
AND TOO MUCH WHISKEY
MAKE A TROUBLED MIND
WANDER TO
RESTLESSLY
ON THE WAY
TO THE INEVITABLE
AND ALL-CONSUMING
EVENTUAL AND LONG-LINGERING
THOUGHTS ABOUT YOU.

...

He wonders ,

Billy does

what happens

when sad lions

get long

in well - gnashed

and once - mighty

teeth

IF YOU'RE READING THIS
YOU KNOW THE REST
BECAUSE CHANCES ARE
WE HAVEN'T TALKED
SINCE YOU MADE
WHAT YOU'RE HOLDING IN YOUR HANDS
THE KIND OF REAL
MY HAND AND THE HOLDING OF
NEVER REALLY COULD BE.

Ruined this too.

latest and last

of the pretty porcelain

finery

unfortunately left

in his China-shop path.

The revelation of
well-repressed
vulnerabilities
left him
the alone he
feared
every single
time.

Fuck You, money

steady waiting on

Fuck You money.

WAIT ...
LEARNING FROM MISTAKES IS A THING
PEOPLE ACTUALLY DO?

Stay

no subtext.

We both know I lied
when I said I can take it.

Baby,
you can't take enough belfies on your
last-year's-model phone

to begin to make it up to me.

Real good at writing
not so much at corresponding

so take this
as a too-late-to-matter
apology

and for the worst of
the lesser well-intentioned words
wasted in the throwing
at you in hopes of

holding onto that little bit of hope
you used to have about me.

...

Reservations are for

restaurants

so fuck it

come over

PART TEN

Inevitable

&

Ill-Timed

Endings

Big Red stays out West
and she never visits
and while she DMs, from time to time,
the time between DMs is getting longer,
like the days,

Spring slowly coming and no immediate
end
to this pandemic or this hell
in sight

and he's losing
sight and in his mind's eye

of the little things,
like what she looked like
and in particular
the look on her pretty little face
back when she used to tell him
she loved him.

She doesn't
love him, or at least tell him,
so much anymore

and maybe the head trauma
does him a favor
in the slow and steady
forgetting
of her face
and
the little details
surrounding the big words

Big Red used to lovingly
say to him.

Doomed doesn't message so much
these days

filled with the longing and regret
that follow
the kind of burning that particular
situation down
the way bad Billy did.

She didn't stay married,
the way they both knew she wouldn't

talks of working on her marriage
believable only in the sense
he got
that she really wanted to
and
that she really tried.

She didn't really
try
and with Billy Ancaster,

and his ill-timed words didn't help,

but Spring is supposedly coming
and Billy Ancaster is grateful for the
warmth of the sun

he'll need to replace
the warmth he used to find
between the lines

in the messages she used to
bother to message him.

Johnny Fucking Ancaster settles down
with Lizzy-Come-Lately,
a surprise to both
Ancasters and
the appropriately named
Lizzy herself.

He's displaying
a remarkable sense of
maturity,
post Flurona

maybe wizening the way
obnoxious Ancasters
seemingly never could

and so his Spring
looks decidedly better than his fall,
full of long walks and
the blunts he can smoke
out on them.

And while Billy is happy for him
he's maybe a little envious, too

and of the companionship
Johnny enjoys and Billy blows up

each and every chance he can,

setting fire to settling

like Johnny sets fire to his next and
appropriately timed

pre-rolled marijuana cigarette.

The Other Married Women stay
married
and
happily *

and
only come around
Brave Billy Ancaster
when it suits their fancy.

So
often
and enough to confuse him
as to both their intentions
and their continued desire
to stay married,

when
staying married
so often leads them
into his rotation
and
on occasion and for some,
into his bed.

Still,
Billy doesn't ask
because Billy doesn't bother

his heart
the broken and decidedly-elsewhere
some pre-married woman took it

way back when she took his hometown.

(*no such thing.)

Ten-Round Tyson is actually
the most stable motherfucker
in this whole book,

married and happily
and father to a litter of
future world title contenders
just like him.

He still boxes,
and Brave Billy,

but head holes and associated trauma
have settled their frequency,

if not their violence

on occasions where
boxing occurs.

So Spring is coming
and looking better
for Ten-Round Tyson,

should the pandemic part
and allow him the free reign
needed to resume

boxing everyone other than
not-doing-so-hot

Brave Billy.

~~Lockdown~~ 4 kind of ends,
kind of doesn't

this "new normal"
anything but
and
never-ending

and
although it has little to do
with the various leavings

burnt out Billy Ancaster
can't help but wonder
if anything can outlast

the sadness he assumes
almost everyone
except the ones who leave him

must most certainly
be left feeling

anxiously awaiting
whatever comes

after lockdown 4
and before

the seemingly inevitable arrival
of fucking lockdown 5.

Gypsy goes off and gets engaged,
Bolivia
or
Venezuela
or
somewhere equally warmer than
here,
the winter Billy Ancaster
waits for word
that she's officially
leaving him, too.

She's happy
and
so he's

--fuck that,
he's not happy about any of it,
or for any of them,

his Spring
coming decidedly darker
than the collective outcome

coming out of the lockdown
described on the previous page

coming for everyone
even remotely associated with him.

So the gypsy goes
the way they all go

--away--

and Billy Ancaster can't even begin to
understand

why and why
he should bother to pretend
to be okay with any of it.

Non Denominational Yearnings aren't

helping

Billy Ancaster deal
with the void
collective leavings
have left him to deal with.

He returns to the things he knows best,

writing

and about the various maladies
currently manifesting themselves
in the corner of his brain
that haven't been
boxed in

and

boxing

and to cope with the various maladies
currently manifesting themselves in the
corner of his brain

Ten-Round Tyson
hasn't beaten to death.

And he's close to death,
Brave Billy,

and he doesn't really realize it,
because that hole in his head

he really should have followed up on,

instead of following up on
the various loves

who couldn't wait to leave him.

Billy Ameaster might make Spring,
but not long after

broken hearts and skulls
taking the toll

broken hearts and skulls
seemingly always tend to,

when tending to neither
result in days following the morning he
maybe doesn't wake up,

fresh off the last
nights

like last night,
the night he tossed and turned

about missing the pretty girls

he misses,

one of which,

*if you're reading this

is most likely

you.

(*it's too late)

THE END

...of brave Billy Ancaster

?

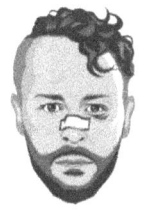

THE END

AND ONLY UNTIL

ANOTHER ONE
MAKES ME WRITE

ANOTHER ONE.

www.ingramcontent.com/pod-product-compliance
Lightning Source LLC
Chambersburg PA
CBHW072154100526
44589CB00015B/2221